# *Surviving Corona*
## *With Humor*

*Souvenir Edition*

ISBN: 978-0-945134-78-7

# Books by Rick Steber

*Rendezvous*
*Traces*
*Union Centennial*
*Where Rolls the Oregon*
*Heartwood*
*Oregon Trail – Last of the Pioneers*
*Roundup*
*New York to Nome*
*Wild Horse Rider*
*Buckaroo Heart*
*No End in Sight*
*Buy the Chief a Cadillac*
*Legacy*
*Forty Candles*
*Secrets of the Bull*
*Caught in the Crosshairs*
*A Promise Given*
*Red White Black*
*All-Around and the 13th Juror*
*A Better Man*
*Three Little Birds*
*Little White Man*
*Fall Down Angel*
*A Cowboy to Love*
*The Outlaw Tobe Skiens*

## Tales of the Wild West Series:
*Oregon Trail, Pacific Coast, Indians, Cowboys,*
*Women of the West, Children's Stories, Loggers,*
*Mountain Men, Miners, Grandpa's Stories,*
*Pioneers, Campfire Stories, Tall Tales,*
*Gunfighters, Grandma's Stories, Western Heroes*

## Wild West Trivia
*Cowboy Trivia, Campfire Trivia, National Parks &*
*Monuments Trivia, Lewis & Clark Trivia, Oregon Trail*
*Trivia and Oregon Trivia (Volumes One & Two)*

## Western Prose & Poems
*Writing the West, Down a Long Dirt Road,*
*Almost There, Seldom Seen*

**www.ricksteber.com**

# *INTRODUCTION*

We each are navigating the threat of Covid-19 in our own way. Many are willing to comply with all the government imposed mandates and directives. They self- quarantine, stay-at-home to save lives, squirt and wash with hand sanitizer, social distance, wear a mask even when they are alone in their car, and believe we are all in this together.

Others in society view the mandates and directives as Constitutional infringements and a classic case of governmental overreach. They feel it is the duty of government to protect their rights and up to each citizen to protect his or her personal health. This group is willing to take their chances against infection by using a common sense approach and going about their normal everyday lives.

If you are reading this – congratulations – it means you are surviving what some have called the worst world-wide pandemic since the Spanish Flu of 1918. Most survivors have discovered the best way to deal with this catastrophic event is to treat it with a sense of humor. To that end, here is a strong dose of Corona humor …. Enjoy, and stay safe.

## SIX FEET APART

I'm so done with it
That we're all in it together
Social distancing, six feet apart
Where's the love, where's the heart

Do you have a fever
Stay at home, save lives
Ride the wave to stay alive
Phase one, two, try to survive

Gonna find me a bar
Ring the bell, buy a round
Listen to the music, listen to the sound
Leave a tip on my tab, play it safe, catch a cab

I miss the hugs
Miss the handshakes too
No school, virtual graduation
How long will it last, crazy situation

Wear a mask, wash your hands
Shelter in place and leave no trace
Hoping like hell there is light after dark
Off in the future when we ain't six feet apart

As the self-ordained Korona Philosopher, I have had plenty of time to contemplate the word "science." People are constantly pointing to that word in an effort to explain how we should behave during this Covid-19 crisis. This is my definition of science: "Science is the intellectual and practical activity encompassing the systematic study of the structure and behavior of the physical and natural world through observation and experiment and is based on information that is currently known. Therefore, science is a 'Best Guess' and is subject to drastic change as new information becomes known."

During this pandamnit, I had a hankerin' for some salsa and went to the Fred Meyer Superstore. I wanted really fresh salsa, but nowhere could I find the date printed on the container. A woman came along and asked if I knew where she could find the Sunshine Honey Mustard Salad Dressing. I told her, "I have no idea. I've been looking and looking and I can't even find a damn date." She replied, "Well cowboy, it's your lucky day, now help me look for that salad dressing."

In the dark days of this pandamnit, I had a conversation with a gal that went something like this. She said, "I want to do something today that will change the world for the better, something significant and lasting. I want to stop all wars and have everyone live in peace and harmony. I want to end hunger, solve global warming, and revolutionize race relations…. You know what? I think I'll change the color of my hair, nothing drastic, just something different."

Back before Corona was even invented—when I was just a boy growing up—to inspire me I suppose—I was told I could someday become President of the United States. In taking a critical look at the political candidates running for that high office, I'm beginning to believe I might actually have a shot at it.

Lately I've been trying to avoid the disturbing news about the uptick in Corona virus cases. Instead I spent time reading about a study that concluded women have better verbal skills than men. I just want to say to the authors of that study: "Duh."

During trying times like these, I think it's important to maintain some sort of normalcy. Today I had my dog sit for a performance evaluation, just to remind him who the hell is still the boss. I'm curious if, during this Covid-19 pandamnit, does opening a bag of pork rinds constitute a complete and full workout?

During the ever-escalating stages of this pandamnit, I have had time to ponder important things. For instance, I have come to the conclusion that high heels must have been invented by a woman who was mistakenly kissed on the forehead.

During this pandamnit, I've come to realize that it is always darkest just before dawn. So I'm here to tell you, if you're gonna steal your neighbor's newspaper, that's the time to do it.

Since this virus crisis hit, I've been forced to stay home without a paycheck. Mostly I occupy my time looking at other peoples' lives on Facebook. Back when I was a kid, having to sit and listen to politics and see photos of what people were eating, their pets and vacations was considered an unjust form of punishment.

## BROODING

Awakened by thoughts
Of the hysteria going on
I step outside into the night
The moon hides behind clouds
A few stars appear like chips of ice
Wind causes the tops of trees to sway
I forget what it was I wanted to tell you
I'm sure it had to do with the wild news of the day
But I doubt if you are even interested
In what it was that I wanted to say
There is a warm orange glow
Coming from the window
Never mind my view
The ground is cool
On my bare feet
Goodnight
Again

I'm just wondering, if we have to endure living through the second season of Corona Virus, do we have to stick with the same boring cast of characters or can we at least switch partners to make it more interesting?

During these dark days in Coronaville, I have constantly been going to doctors and having them test me for the virus. One thing I have determined is to never employ a doctor where all the plants in the office are … dead.

Just once in my life I would like to meet an honest politician who refuses to try and answer a question on the grounds he/she does not know the answer.

I was thankful the local swimming pool opened for the summer even if, due to social distancing, there was no water in lanes two, four and six.

NEWS FLASH FROM 2015: Not a single person answered the question correctly – "Where do you see yourself in five years?"

I'm planning on saving a lot of money this Christmas by telling the kids the sad news that, although Santa fought valiantly, he wasn't able to survive the terrible Covid-19 pandamnit....

Because of Covid-19 and the wearing of masks and social distancing, the National Spelling Bee has officially been cancaled… canculed … canseled … oh hell, the event has been called off….

THIS JUST IN from the scientific community: Scientists have declared it's an absolute fact that if you stick your tongue on an outdoor bug zapper you will be immune from contracting Covid-19.

The World Health Organization (WHO) has announced that dogs have a natural immunity and cannot contract Covid-19. They have ordered all dogs being held in quarantine to immediately be released … and now it's pretty damn obvious WHO let the dogs out.

## LIFE IS A MOUNTAIN

Been my experience
Every mountain has two sides
One is hidden and the other in full view

One is for climbing, one step at a time
The other is for sliding down
Which you choose is strictly up to you

When we begin
Life is something
We take for granted

One step after another
Seeking out our groove
Always reaching upward

Life upon this mountain
Is the only life we shall ever know
Keep climbing even when the going gets slow

Sometimes we seek forgiveness
For our careless missteps along the way
Just give it your best shot on any given day

When you finally reach the lofty summit
And your name rings out loud and clear
Slide with style, grace and good cheer

During the fear and panic stage of this government sponsored virus crisis, I've been studying ways to improve myself. One thing I read was that everyone has a purpose in life. I'm beginning to think my purpose might be to watch all 2,384 episodes of *Family Feud* hosted by Steve Harvey.

As the Korona Philosopher, I've been reviewing a lot of amazing inventions—from radio to television, from airplanes to space travel—but for my money, the greatest invention of all time has to be the digital camera. The digital camera allows us to reminisce instantly.

The mask people, six-feet-awayers, and the constant hand-sanitizers … boy oh boy are they ever gonna feel stupid someday when they are lying in a hospital bed dying of absolutely nothing.

The Corona virus keeps reminding us that we are all in this together. I've tried to keep in touch with others by using ZOOM. The trouble is, I almost hate to tell a good story about something important or interesting or funny that happened to me because it always reminds one of the others of some incredibly dull story they feel compelled to tell.

A married couple I know has taken this Corona virus very seriously. They stay at home, comply with the six feet mandate and even sleep in separate rooms. The have dinner apart, watch TV apart and the few times they venture out they always take separate cars. As far as I can tell, during these difficult times, they are doing everything they can to make their marriage work.

This Corona virus has really knocked our economy on its butt. But even in these difficult times I remain positively optimistic. I believe that if life gives you lemons, you should make lemonade, and do your damnedest to find somebody whose life has given them vodka, and then the two of you can have one hell of a party.

I've been very diligent about living in harmony with all the mandates and have remained at home while the government pays me unemployment. Today my dad made a point to tell me that hard work never killed anybody. I told him, "Yeah, well maybe that's true, but why take a chance?"

For months during this crisis I have stayed home and didn't venture out. Only recently have I started driving again. What I have noticed is that anybody driving slower than me is an absolute idiot, and anyone going faster is a maniac.

While I have all this extra Corona time on my hands, I've been spending it writing a book in fifth person. Every sentence of dialogue begins with: "I heard this from a guy who told somebody's third cousin, and he told a friend who told a friend to tell me...."

## FEARLESS

I ain't never gonna die from a life unlived
I refuse to safety up with guarantees
I wanna be risky and fearless
Challenging myself

Give me freedom
To inhabit places
Away from others
Who try to limit my
Wandering ways
And my capacity
To think freely

I am a tiny seedling
That reaches ever skyward
Tasting the rapture of sun and soil
To bloom, bear fruit and make a difference

Most folks seem to meekly comply with the mandates: stay-at-home, mask-up, social distance, we are all in this together, go along and get along. As a result some people suffer from anxiety issues and mental stress. Some choose alcohol or to medicate themselves with drugs sold by the state. On a personal level, I've come to the conclusion I can resist almost everything except for maybe temptation.

The government mandates and directives had me doubting myself. I began to lack self-confidence and reached a point where I thought perhaps I might be indecisive. Now I'm not so sure about that....

My new girlfriend and I play by all the Covid rules. During this prolonged odyssey we have stayed home and remained unemployed. The other night she confided she suffers from kleptomania. I suspected that all along because she takes everything so literally.

While trapped in the Covid-19 spiral, I made an important discovery. What I discovered was that whenever I misplace the television controller, it's always hidden in some remote location.

"I catch a little shut-eye, wake up and everyone is wearing masks. I thought only outlaws wore masks. People avoid me like the plague and if I get too close they hiss at me and say, 'Six-feet, six-feet.' …. What the hell is going on here?" … (Rip Van Winkle)

During this era of no-school/home-school, it has come to my attention that if you want your children to actually listen to you, all you have to do is start talking softly to someone else.

Have you ever known someone you would consider to be two-faced? If so, answer me this—during this virus crisis, and keeping in strict compliance with the governor's mandate—would that person be required to wear a mask on both faces?

I've had my fair share of dealing with lawyers, and since this Corona virus came along I've listened to the opinion of a plethora of so-called expert physicians. In my humble opinion, lawyers and doctors are cut from the same bolt of cloth. The only difference is, lawyers will rob you, and doctors will rob you and kill you too.

The Korona Philosopher strikes again—You know, I look around at my world and realize the behavior of a crocodile is rather predictable. It's an animal that wants to kill and eat you. On the other hand, people are harder to predict. Sometimes they first pretend to be your friend.

## WALKING THE DOG

During the Covid crisis
When out walking my dog
One thing I have recently noticed
I have an opportunity to meet a lot of dogs

With this pandamnit and social unrest running wild, we are all being forced to live in constant fear. Now to top it off the government says we need to worry about terrorism. But I'm not scared. Not one little bit. After all, at one time I was married.

This self-isolation mandated by the governor—forcing me to wear a mask so I look exactly like everybody else, and having to stay six feet away from people—well, it all got to me. I started feeling sorry for myself and thought nobody cares if I live or die. Then I missed a car payment, house payment and forgot about the electric and water bills and discovered there are a lot of people who care about me.

No need for you to be so outrageously concerned about the Corona virus pandamnit. If you wanna worry about something take a long look at obesity. According to the National Institutes of Health, obesity causes 300,000 preventable deaths each year. As you digest that bit of information, please pass the potatoes and gravy….

During this Corona stay-at-home policy, I've been reading a lot of autobiographies. I think a law should be passed that a person cannot write their autobiography until after they're dead.

After the government gets done throwing money at the Corona virus we will end up with runaway inflation. Just so you know, inflation is when you pay thirty dollars for the fifteen-dollar haircut you used to get for five bucks back when you had hair.

I was listening to the director of the Health Authority speak at a press conference about the terrible effects of the virus crisis. During the interview he stated, "I don't want to be surrounded by 'yes' people. I want everybody to tell me the truth, even if it ends up costing them their job."

During this forced time at home I've completed a lot of projects. The other day I painted my picket fence. Why do people automatically believe masks save lives and social distancing is the answer, but they have to check for themselves when they see a sign that reads "Wet Paint"?

I believe everything the medical community and the governor tell me. I live in mortal fear of catching the Corona virus and have sequestered myself away from friends and society. Last night I was reading a book by Helen Keller. She was an American author, political activist, and lecturer and the first deaf-blind person to earn a Bachelor of Arts degree. In the text I read a quote by Helen Keller – "Avoiding danger is no safer in the long run than outright exposure. The fearful are caught as often as the bold." …. Now I don't know who the hell to believe.

The governor declared the calendar factory where I work an essential business. I was happy about that and thought I had it made. Then I got fired. I can't believe I got fired. All I did was take off one lousy day.

## SEARCHING FOR ALLEGORY

In this state of mortal combat
We set up night guards to protect us
Send out scouts to avoid walking into traps
Avoid passing too close to any lake
To circumvent being ambushed

Wind whistles through the pine needles
The scent of rain hangs heavy
We avoid river crossings
For the enemy will be watching
If we ever identify our enemy we will fight

I refuse to be a follower … unless it's a really dark night and we're lost, then I want you to go first….

So, the experts are claiming this Corona virus might be our Armageddon. Even though I don't have any idea what "Armageddon" means, I'm damn sure it ain't the end of the world.

I've been diligently studying history, while staying home vegetating and saving thousands of lives by not being inconsiderate and spreading the terrible corona virus, I read the biography of Ponce de León and his search for the Fountain of Youth. That got me wondering if, out there somewhere, there might be a Fountain of Stop Being So Damn Stupid.

During this Corona crisis, peer pressure requires me to put on a mask before going out in public. But yesterday I went for a walk without my mask. Suddenly I found myself in the middle of a mob of angry protesting clowns. To save myself, I went straight for the juggler.

During this Corona-inspired crisis I discovered a man can be cooped up for only so long and then he has to get outside. Yesterday I decided to do some yardwork, but when I checked my glove drawer all I could find were 'lefties.' On one hand that was great, but on the other, it just ain't right.

During this government-imposed virus crises, I've chosen to sequester myself in my tiny apartment. But I still make phone calls. The other day I got into a lengthy discussion on the phone with a friend about whether or not orthopedic shoes would help my foot problem. I really didn't think they would, but now I stand corrected.

For the past three months I've been strictly adhering to the governor's directive to stay at home, stop working and be content to draw unemployment. My recreation consists of drinking alcohol and watching the hands on the clock. After untold hours of study, I have come to the conclusion that 6:30 is the best time on a clock, hands down.

With the stay-at-home order fully in place, I've had a lot of down time. I picked up a bible and started reading it. I came to the conclusion that Adam and Eve were probably the first on the planet to completely ignore Apple terms and conditions.

Three guys wearing masks and maintaining acceptable social distancing walk into a bar. Damn, I thought at least one of them would have seen it.

### *JUST LIVING*

Let's get real here
Boil it down to just you
A tent, bedroll and a campfire
Out in the deep woods somewhere
A long ways from where you are now
Near a river, under a scattering of stars
Just leave behind all your rowdy mortality
And for once in a very long time choose living

I will admit, since I've been ordered to not leave my house because of this Corona virus, I've gained a few extra pounds. But having spent time researching, I've learned, if I was lucky enough to live on the planet Mercury, I'd weigh about half what I do on Earth. My conclusion is, I'm on the wrong damn planet.

I'm in a real dilemma and need some guidance. When this government/media inspired pandamnit is over, which meeting should I attend first, Weight Watchers or Alcoholics Anonymous?

As the Korona Philosopher it has occurred to me that I was born to make mistakes, but certainly not to try and fake perfection.

It used to be the rule, that for the sake of good mental health, it was important to stay away from negative people. The Corona virus has changed that. Now we have to avoid positive people.

We are now living in Coronaville and what a crazy place this is. The real irony is that when Dad gets caught sneaking out of his house, it's his kids yelling at him to stay indoors.

No schools and virtual learning has me concerned about our future. Do you realize that in about the year 2040 the political power in the United States is gonna reside in the hands of kids who were home schooled by a bunch of day-drinking parents?

This Corona virus has accomplished what no woman has ever been able to do—cancel all sports, shut down the bars and keep men at home working on their honey-do lists.

Before this virus crisis it never occurred to me that the old saying, "I won't touch her with a six-foot pole," would actually become a national policy.

I asked Alexa to tell me the weather report for the weekend. The voice rang out loud and clear, "What the hell does it matter? You ain't goin' nowhere. You're quarantined."

## TURN THE PAGE

I know a man
Who reads his newspaper
As it was intended to be read
Turning pages, folding them back

He has very little interest
In stock market ups and downs
Or the current fluctuations of gold
Turning always to one particular section

Short reports on the thinning of the herd
Names are listed there of the dearly departed
Who leave only air to rush in where they once stood
He reads it all: age, the cause, and their accomplishments

Each item dutifully noted
Black ink on cheap white paper
This one built bird houses from scrap wood
Another had a world class collection of Native dolls

Reaching the end of the solemn page
He adds it all up in his head to discover
Nearly half were younger than he is now
He gives thanks and goes on about his day

This Corona virus has me all mixed up in the head. For one thing, I've been gaining weight, maybe thirty pounds, so I made up my mind to go on a very strict tequila diet. It seems to be working. I've already lost three days.

While forced to stay at home, I've been exploring options for new hobbies and discovered I might be interested in skydiving. But when I read how much it costs, that turned me off a little. Then it occurred to me I could save money by not buying a parachute. After all, you really don't need a parachute to go skydiving unless you plan to go skydiving a second time.

In these dark days of the Corona virus most everything we eat is takeout food. Contrast that to when I was a kid growing up. My family's menu consisted of two choices: eat it or starve.

Personally, if I've learned anything from this pandamnit, it's to take what the government and the media says with a grain of salt. I also have found it rather helpful to add a slice of lemon and a shot or two or three of tequila.

This government/media induced virus-crises has made me aware of both knowledge and wisdom. As far as I'm concerned, knowledge is in knowing something important—like that a tomato is a fruit—and wisdom is in never adding tomatoes to a fruit salad.

I read all the Corona virus predictions the same way I read science fiction. When I get to the end, I think, "Well, most of this crap ain't gonna happen anyway."

During this lengthy stay-at-home directive, I've become very skeptical of those who tell me they are spending an hour a day doing yoga. Personally I find that to be a bit of a stretch.

Isn't it interesting that everyone automatically assumes a hand sanitizer dispenser is filled with hand sanitizer? I like to fill my dispenser with mustard to give my friends a lesson in trust.

While I've been staying at home, drawing unemployment and saving lives, I've been playing computer chess. The computer beats me nearly every time, but I discovered that computer is no match for me when it comes to kickboxing.

## TRUTH

I watch a woman hang laundry
On a line to dry in wind and sun

I see the surgeon stop for coffee
And buy a maple bar
On his way to the operating room

I witness neither of these dramas
As they are unfolding in time

Nor can I imagine the surgeon
Opening the chest of a man
To fix a leaky heart valve

Or the woman opening a telegram
Notification her soldier son is dead

None of this is true
But it could all be true
What can we ever believe

When the governor started opening up the economy, I was forced to give up my unemployment and go back to work. Today my boss announced he was going to lay off the employee with the worst posture. I have a hunch it might be me.

Since the government furloughed all but "essential" workers, I've completed a host of home-improvement projects. Most people are really shocked when they find out how bad I am as an electrician.

The governor demanded I stay at home. I have to exercise on my own rather than go to the gym and I am doing a lot of my own cooking. Today I burned 4,000 calories. That's the last time I leave brownies in the oven while I take a nap.

The governor has been telling all of us, if we want to keep from getting the terrible Corona virus we need to stay at home and keep both feet firmly on the ground. But I've found, if I do that, it is really difficult to pull on my pants.

All this social distancing made me wish for the good old days—handshakes and hugs—and that got me thinking about nostalgia. I wonder how long that word has been around.

I have a friend who has become so absolutely obsessed with news about the Corona virus that she was considering having a brain transplant, but then she changed her mind.

During the virus crisis I've been a good little boy and tried to do my recreating at home. Trapped like I am, I've come to the conclusion there is no such thing as an actual addiction, there are only things you enjoy doing more than living your lousy damn stay-at-home life.

The slogan we've all been beaten over the head with—we are all in this together—got me thinking, and I want you to know, if we are in a boat on the ocean and we start taking on water and there is only one life jacket, I promise to say only nice things about you.

During this stay-at-home directive, my therapist has been treating me via Zoom. Just the other day I was visiting with her from my tree fort and she told me, "You have a lot of growing up to do."

## PASSING CORONA TIME

I carefully examine the ceiling
With cracks like rivers
Time dies slowly
Plaster flakes

I remain inert
Upon this couch
Lost in mindless thought
As the room breathes in and out

Due to the Corona virus, I've had a lot of extra time on my hands. I got to remembering back years ago and that old song about the guy who didn't know much about history, or geography, or the French he took. He must be the one who came up with the word "necking" because he obviously knew nothing about human anatomy.

During this prolonged pandemic, the couple was buying takeout from various restaurants. After finishing their meal from a Chinese restaurant, the husband and wife cracked open their fortune cookies. Her fortune read, "Be quiet for a little while." His read, "Talk while you have the chance."

During this pandamnit, more people than ever have started reading again. Yesterday I had someone tell me the things they love most about reading are turning pages and the smell of a book. My reply was, "Apparently you have no real idea how this reading thing actually works."

During pandamnit I've been working out with weights and running religiously—I did once at Easter and I plan to do so again at Christmas.

With all this time on my hands I got thinking about the board game Monopoly. Can you tell me why only one company is allowed to make that popular game?

During this era of social distancing, some of my friends and I broke the law and got together to play games. I'm here to attest to the fact that the absolute worst time to have a heart attack is during a spirited game of charades.

I thought maybe I had contracted the Corona virus, so I went to the doctor and he discovered I'm color blind. Wow, that diagnosis came completely out of the purple.

It was the height of insanity when the government forced Starbucks to close, deeming coffee was not essential. Now Starbucks has announced they are opening with social distancing and will print religious quotes on cups. The very first quote should be, 'Jesus! This cup of coffee is expensive!'

During this stay-at-home directive, I was surprised to have a man knock on my door and ask for a donation on behalf of the local swimming pool. I wasn't sure what my appropriate response should be, so I gave him a glass of warm water.

## DRAWING YOU

I have no talent for art it would seem
And yet I decided to draw you
Don't ask my why I chose
Something so difficult

Your cheek bones
Prominent and lovely
Do they start at your nose
Or somewhere along the way

Trying my best to remember
The river flow of your hair
How your lips purse to
Pout or to smile

How can I ever hope to capture
The blue light flickering in your eyes
You have been away such a very long time
It will all come back to me if I ever see you again

My girlfriend and I have been quarantined in this tiny apartment, living in mortal fear of catching the virus. Last night she started this huge rant about how I never listen to her…. Anyway, I think she was saying something along that line….

I used to have an imaginary friend. I really liked my imaginary friend. But I had to get rid of her because she refused to wear a mask and social distance.

During this pandamnit I keep hearing we are all in this together. The other thing people tell me—to try and build up my self-confidence I suppose—is that nothing is impossible. But without a job I do nothing every damn day.

Virus crisis or no virus crisis one thing is clear—people want to live. If everyone didn't wanna live then tell me why, back in World War Two, did kamikaze pilots bother to wear helmets?

As the Korona Philosopher it has occurred to me that men generally marry women with the hope they will be wild and crazy and never change. On the other hand, a woman generally marries a man with the hope she can change that man's bad behavior. Invariably both sexes are disappointed.

I've been listening to the politicians and health care experts discuss the pandamnit. The conclusion I have come to is the real difference between stupidity and genius is that genius has definite limits.

What if this global pandamnit is simply God's way of trying to teach Americans about world geography….

We seem so caught up in Corona virus, protests and riots in the cities that we have lost sight of the fact we need to spend billions on schools, bridges and roads, but right now that money is desperately needed for more political ads.

I've survived a lot in my life—recessions, depressions, governmental overreach and the latest is the Corona virus and the host of forced mandates—and I have to say that, in my learned opinion, the average dog is way nicer than the average person.

## LOCKDOWN

Trying to find life
Under the heavy shadow
Of a stay-at-home directive

Bathroom window
Looks out on a garden
Cloaked in a layer of snow
All prospects of spring hiding

Ivy clings to cinder blocks
A yellow metal table stands idle
As does a wood chair pulled up tight
Useless old thing with one wonky leg

Each morning of this mandated exile
A noisy bird flutters against the window
Perching on a bare-boned branch it squawks
While a woman soaks in the tub under pale light

Submerged in soapy water up to her neck
She wonders what outfit she should wear today
Knowing it really doesn't matter one way or another
She will be alone and without any prospects of company

During this long pandamnit I've begun exploring astrology. What I've discovered is that I really can't believe in all that hokus pokus. You know, I'm a Scorpio and we're always skeptical about things like that.

I didn't believe the Corona virus was any worse than the flu. Then I did. I thought maybe masks and social distancing were helpful, and now I don't. My opinions may change, but not the fact that I'm always right.

I used to be an introvert, but along came Covid-19 and I've learned to stand up and say what I think. Now I try to be who I am and say what I feel. What I've found is that those who mind don't matter and those who matter don't mind.

I watch all the political news, the unrest in the big cities and the daily updates on the Corona virus and that got me to thinking about aliens. I think that the surest sign intelligent life exists elsewhere in the universe is that aliens have never gone out of their way to try and contact us in any obvious way.

When it comes to Covid-19 you have two sides of the fence—the mask people and the non-conformists, the social distance people and the close talkers. I'm a tolerant man and my motto is to never judge another man until I've walked a mile in his boots. After that who cares? I'm a mile away and I've got his boots.

I sit here alone, away from any possible contact with the dreaded Corona virus. I know that somewhere inside me there's a thin person struggling to get out. I'm thankful I can usually sedate him with a half-dozen cupcakes.

I don't mind that during this pandamnit some people laugh at me for wearing rubber gloves, face mask and a dunce cap. After all, throughout history many true geniuses were laughed at. Columbus was laughed at by the flatlanders. The Wright Brothers were laughed at by those who thought man could never fly. But lately I've come to appreciate the fact that people also laugh at Bozo the Clown.

I hate that the governor has the power to close down the gym where I usually go five days a week. That really breaks my heart because, at the gym, my favorite machine of all time is the vending machine.

I listen to the doomsday reporters on television news claiming the world is about to come to an end today. But I'm not the least bit concerned. After all, it's already tomorrow in Australia.

## BLACK VELVET ELVIS

Hunkered down here all alone
Waiting for the virus to hit me
All I have are four lonely walls
Girl with no eyes is staring at me
My pride and joy, black velvet Elvis

We gotta do this and do it right now
Six-feet away, practice proper hygiene
Wash your hands at least 50 times a day
News tells me, sure as hell I'm gonna die
Hoard the TP and it's NO on reusable bags

Germs fly in the sky while the general public
Navigates paved city streets in foreign-made cars
Fearing Bigfoot and that invading army from Mars
While the Corona virus sends us quaking to our knees
Black velvet Elvis come and save us, come save us all

The governor urges anyone who plans on dying from some preexisting condition in the immediate future to please contact the Health Authority so they can make sure and expose you to covid-19. Be part of the crime, not the cure.

Since we entered the time-warp of Coronaville, I've been devoting my time to exploring various intellectual theories. One theory holds that if we all, collectively, came to understand exactly what the Universe is for and why it is here, it will instantly disappear and be replaced by something even more bizarre and inexplicable. There is another theory which states this has already happened. Welcome to 2020.

I've been a good boy and followed all the directives issued by the governor to her loyal subjects. I stayed at home, self-quarantined and cashed my unemployment checks right on schedule. I did everything to be socially conscious and save lives. Yesterday I put on my mask and went to play alone in a park. I threw my Frisbee and stood there intently watching it. I wondered why the Frisbee seemed to be getting bigger and bigger and bigger … and then it hit me.

During the virus crisis it has occurred to me that trying to analyze humor is a bit like dissecting a frog. Few people are interested and the frog is already dead.

I was using my "stay at home—save lives" time to write a novel. I figure another six months and I will have it finished. Then it suddenly hit me, why spend a year writing a novel when I can go to the library book sale and buy all the novels I want for a buck each.

With the election infection, civil unrest and rioting, I have come to the conclusion that true happiness is in having a large, loving, caring, close-knit family living in another state.

During these dark days of the pandamnit, a new survey has been conducted by our state government which showed that 93% of all men say their lover is also their best friend. What makes this even more disturbing is when you consider man's best friend has always been his dog.

Socially conscious of all the virus mandates as I am, and even wearing a mask when I am alone in my car, I have observed that Americans are undoubtedly the most incredibly impatient people on the face of our planet. The shortest period of time in America is between when the light turns green and when you hear the first horn honk.

This Covid-19 crisis has turned me into a two-bit philosopher. My latest observation is that we're rarely aware of the bullets we dodge. The just-misses. The almost-never-happeneds. We spend so much time worrying about how the future is going to play out that we rarely spend time admiring the precious perfection of the present.

## NOTHING MUCH

It seems today there is nothing much to write about
Except perhaps for sickness, life and death
That and the solitary sound of a train
Blowing its whistle at the crossing
A lonely and desperate sound
That echoes across miles

If I were on that night train
I could write of lights flashing past
Of moonlight and cattle grazing on pasture
Using straight lines to indicate our amazing speed
As the locomotive pulls me closer and closer to home
All the while speed lines trailing out behind our madcap rush

During this pandamnit I've been reading a ton of health journals. I now realize that by reading every word, and believing every word, there's a pretty good chance I'll die of a misprint.

I listen to all the mandates issued by our governor, directing us how we should act. It is my belief we need fewer stupid people and more geniuses with humility; after all there are so few of us left.

As the Korona Philosopher I dream of a better tomorrow, a world where chickens can cross the road and not be questioned about their motives.

Trying to date during this time of Covid is nearly impossible—no bars, restaurants or movie theatres. I just hope when I do eventually meet Miss Right, her first name will not be "Always".

A friend of mine got the horrible Corona virus. His doctor gave him six months to live, but when he couldn't pay the bill, the doctor gave him six months more.

During these dark days of this pandamnit, social unrest, riots, shootings, political bickering and all the rest, it suddenly occurred to me that common sense and humor are basically the same thing. Humor is just common sense, dancing.

This media-inspired virus crisis and government lockdown has given me way too much time on my hands. I've been thinking about things that don't really matter to a hill of beans. For instance, last night I got to wondering what would happen to a parsley farmer if he didn't pay his taxes. Could the IRS garnish him?

Because of this pandamnit, the governor informed me I wasn't essential to society. I was sent home without a paycheck, no unemployment compensation or anything else to sustain my economic well-being. But I'm not worried. I have my savings. In fact I have all the money I'll ever need—as long as I'm willing to die before dinnertime today.

Here we are, something like day six thousand into this pandamnit and I finally ventured out of my stay-at-home apartment. As I was driving along looking for a yard sale, I happened upon a sign reading, 'Watch for Children,' and I thought to myself, you know, that sounds like a pretty fair trade.

# NEWS

The television flickers blue
With news of preachers
Having fallen from grace

Telling of the misdeeds
Of national politicians
And more mass shootings

Virus spreading out of control
Fear sets in; panic prevails
Will your neighbor be the next

While in my remote corner
Of this broad world
The Bible is read religiously

Clothes are pinned to sagging lines
Old men thumb the almanac
Trying to gauge the severity of winter

Nobody around these parts
Pays much attention to
The antics of television news

This stay-at-home policy can be difficult on a relationship. Just last night I told my girlfriend I thought she was drawing her eyebrows a little too high. Boy, did she ever look surprised.

During this pandamnit I was killing time reading the dictionary. What I came across on one page was absolutely disgraceful, disgusting, dishonest, and disingenuous.

Lately, since I haven't been able to work, I've had a little too much time on my hands. Well anyway, last night I was wondering why it is that I've never seen newspaper headlines that read, "Psychic Wins Hundred Million Dollar Lottery."

During the Corona Crisis, civil unrest, election counts, lock-downs, lock-outs and lock-ups, I have tried to keep an open mind about things. I realize that by keeping an open mind, there is a fairly good chance my brains will all fall out.

I have to admit to the fact that when I was growing up I always wanted to be SOMEBODY. Now, with the wisdom of being the Korona Philosopher, I realize I should have been more specific.

Having to try and endure this Corona lockdown with kids in the house, it occurred to me that cleaning up with children around is like shoveling snow during a blizzard.

During this stay-at-home directive we are forced to get along. My significant other claimed she wanted a puppy to help her get through these troubled times. But I put my foot down and said absolutely not. I don't want a puppy. So we compromised and she got a puppy.

I'm trying to make sure not to lose my cognitive skills during this government-imposed staycation. So I was trying to remember what I know about Pavlov. He was that Russian physiologist best know for his work in classical conditioning. And then I got to wondering what would happen if Pavlov walked into a bar and the phone rang. Would Pavlov suddenly announce, "Damn, I forgot to feed the dog."

Perhaps I've spent too much time alone, but I'm hoping someone can help me with this. I'm just wondering, at what age do you think it's appropriate to tell a highway it's adopted?

## THE MOMENT

I realize I am a dragonfly
With twenty-four hours to live
A soap bubble floating in the woods

At the La Brea Tar Pits
Standing under the bones
Of a long extinct dinosaur

Understanding that anyone
Who has stood at the brink of time
Is momentarily cheating the inevitable

Seeing those white crosses
Pulled tight against the roadway
Is to appreciate the fine art of dying

There are so many reminders
Of my short span of mortality
Here but for a brief moment

I was visiting with a liberal acquaintance who willingly complies with all of the governor's mandates and directives. From behind a mask this person actually told me, "I intend to live forever, and so far, so good."

During this time of Coronaville, I decided to work real hard at self-discipline and getting myself in the peak of condition. I became dedicated to jogging, but had to give it up. The ice cubes in my "refreshment" kept bouncing out of the glass.

Covid has reminded me that the only way to keep your health is to eat what you don't want, drink what you don't like, and do those things you don't wanna do.

Because of this pandamnit, I've had a few anxiety issues and started seeking professional help. Just the other day my therapist told me he thinks I have a preoccupation with vengeance. I told him, "Well buddy, you sure as hell are gonna see about that."

All spring I was shut away at home hiding from the Corona virus. Now that summer is here I have vowed to quit eating and drinking, get myself in shape, and enjoy the sun before the rainy season arrives once again. You are my witness. I hereby promise to eat less, get out and exercise more, and number three – what was I talking about? I'm hungry and thirsty. Believe I'll have a beer and a burger....

I finally ventured out from where I have been quarantined at home, only to discover how absolutely ironic it is that the colors red, white, and blue are supposed to stand for freedom; until red, white and blue lights flash in your rearview mirror.

THIN ICE RULE: I found this to be true—whenever I'm skating on thin ice, the only thing that is gonna keep me safe is to skate really, really fast.

What makes me happy during this pandamnit is when I sit at home, evening shadows coming on, and I listen to the sweet music of children laughing and playing in my backyard ... unless I've been drinking and then it will hit me that I'm not married and I don't have children.

Ever since the government shut down businesses amid the virus crisis, I've found that when I go to buy toilet paper, hamburger meat or grapes, it's my money doing all the talking, and what it says is—goodbye.

## *MISS SMILE*

Masks disturb me
Those eyes staring
Such awkward fear

Eyes that watch
Way too much news
Concern leads to panic

What I really miss most of all
Is to look at a stranger's face
And see those lips smile

With all the crap that's going on in the United States, it got me to pondering the vast difference between ignorance and apathy. My conclusion is, I don't have an opinion and really don't give a damn.

Don't you just hate it when some smarty pants know-it-all expert like Doctor Fauci answers his own questions? I know I sure as hell do.

Fear seems to be the trigger point with this virus crisis. Fear of getting Covid-19. Fear that someone will pass it on to you. Fear of stepping outside your home. Fear of touching anything with a germ. I know all about fear. I'm deathly afraid of spiders. Once I saw a spider in my bathroom. I grabbed a wad of toilet tissue and proceeded to burned down my house.

The government closed down restaurants for inside dining, but then allowed limited outside/inside dining. I'm thinking of opening a restaurant strictly for politicians. It will be called Karma. There will be no menu and every politician will get exactly what he/she deserves.

If the germaphobes don't get out and expose themselves to a few germs they are not going to build antibodies and will die prematurely. When that happens, who the hell will be around for me to argue with?

I was talking to my neighbor over the fence. We were very mindful of maintaining the government-imposed Corona six-foot rule. He told me and I quote, "My father has schizophrenia, but he's really good people."

I know what they are saying—that we are all in this together—but sometimes letting go of someone is the only way to survive a mountain climbing catastrophe.

Watching the death count climb on the virus pandamnit, it occurred to me that the best job in the world has to belong to a coroner. What's the worst thing that could happen? If everything goes to hell, a corpse might have a pulse.

I've just been killing time during the Corona stay-at-home directive and feeling pretty dang proud of myself. The puzzle I've been working on reads three to five years, but hell, I finished it in only two months.

## UNFETTERED SKY

Recently I have come to a point of awareness
On the lack of air passengers on the move
Polished planes traipsing north – south
Sometimes I will look off westward
View the snowcapped outlines
Of lofty mountain peaks
Unfettered by streaks
Contrails of vapor
Stripes on sky
Thank you
Covid-19
The end

Doing nothing during this stay-at-home directive you may be feeling lazy. But just know, as lazy as you may feel, you will never be as lazy as the people who came up with the name fireplace, dishwasher or mixer.

With all this extra time on my hands during this pandamnit, I got to thinking about the days of the Wild West. I believe that a lot of the conflict occurring on a dusty street—men with blazing six-shooters—could have been avoided had architects in those days simply made towns big enough for both of us.

When a Covid-19 vaccine has been distributed, and you find yourself looking for a job, always tell the interviewer you're willing and able to give 110 percent—unless you happen to be applying for a job as a statistician.

While we are under this stay-at-home directive my girlfriend and I often laugh about how competitive the two of us are. But I think I laugh way more than she does.

The stay-at-home-save-lives mandate finally got to me and I felt overwhelmed and needed to escape. I went to a nearby park, threw my boomerang. It never came back. Now I live in constant fear.

As the nation moves steadily down the road to socialism, I was hoping the government would provide every citizen with a bicycle. Since that hasn't happened, I decided to ask God for a bike. But I know God doesn't really work that way. So I went out and stole a bike. On Sunday I'll go to confession and ask for forgiveness.

During this pandamnit I've had to eliminate going to monthly meetings of several organizations I belong to because the members refuse to wear masks and respect social distancing. I joined a new group called, "Do the Right Thing" with the hope the meetings would adhere to the governor's strict directives. Now I'm not so sure. When I walked in the room I was told to line up alphabetically according to my height.

I read all the reports about the virus crisis and the political and social upheaval in America and wish I could do something. But I'm so small. How could one insignificant person ever make a difference? Then I spent a night in a tent trying to sleep with a mosquito on the loose.

I was watching a Corona virus update on the local news and the newscaster stated that laughing at our mistakes can lengthen our lives. I appreciate that. But I also know from personal experience that if I laugh at someone's mistake it can drastically shorten my life.

## CORONA

Six feet is my personal space
Howard Hughes come save the day
Wash your hands, wash 'em once again
Wear a mask to keep the Boogieman at bay

This ain't as simple
As the common cold
Way more deadly than the flu
Sure as hell this monkey is gonna get you

Keep the kids at home, outta school
Stop going to work, but run to Walmart
Buy a case of toilet paper; no, make it three
Yet the only thing getting wiped is public gatherings

Chicken Little Syndrome
The sky is falling! The sky is falling!
Henny-Penny don't go down in the burrow
But tell me where to go when the volcano blows

Panic and hysteria
Gotta add to the fear
But as far as I am concerned
I liked it best when Corona was a beer

Rick Steber, the author of more than fifty books and sales of two million copies, has received national acclaim for his writing. His numerous awards include the Western Writers of America Spur Award for Best Western Novel, Independent Publishers Award— Best Regional Fiction, Western Heritage Award, Benjamin Franklin Award, Mid-America Publishers Award, Oregon Library Association Award and Oregon Literary Arts Award. Five of his books have been optioned to movie production companies.

In addition to his writing, Rick is an engaging Western personality and has the unique ability to make his characters come alive as he tells a story. He has spoken at national and international conferences and visits schools where he talks to students about the importance of education, developing reading and writing skills, and impressing upon them the value of saving our history for future generations.

Rick has two sons, Seneca and Dusty. He lives near Prineville, Oregon and writes in a cabin in the timbered foothills of the Ochoco Mountains.